THE UNOFFICIAL
STAR WARS—INSPIRED
BOOK OF COCKTAILS

THE UNOFFICIAL

STAR WARS–INSPIRED
BOOK OF COCKTAILS

Drinks from a Bar Far, Far Away

RHIANNON LEE

PHOTOGRAPHY BY GEORGIE GLASS

Skyhorse Publishing

Visit our website at www.skyhorsepublishing.com.

10 9 8 7 6 5 4 3 2

Library of Congress Cataloging-in-Publication Data is available on file.

Cover design by David Ter-Avanesyan
Cover photo by Georgie Glass

Print ISBN: 978-1-5107-6895-6
Ebook ISBN: 978-1-5107-6896-3

Printed in the United States of America

*Special thanks to Sophie McNamara,
a Jedi Master when it comes to cocktail styling.*

*Thanks also to Tecwyn and Andy who showed great patience
in indoctrinating me into the Star Wars Universe.*

Finally, thanks to Mark, the always-willing cocktail tester.

THE JEDI COCKTAIL CODE

All those who partake in the libations within this sacred text must
be of legal drinking age on their planet of origin. Those found in
possession of this book who are not of age will be exiled to the mining
planet of Kessel in the Outer Rim for fifty years of hard labor under
the rule of the mighty Galactic Empire.

All cocktails featured in this book have been certified and tested for
Human, Hutt, and Togruta consumption. None of the following
recipes have been tested on adorable fluffy life forms such as Ewoks
or Wookiees. Therefore, please proceed with caution if serving any
cocktails to hairy mumbling party guests, as side effects may vary.

Those who are wise and have chosen to follow the path to become a
Jedi Master of Mixology must learn the necessary balance of fortified
spirits. The secret to creating a great cocktail is in the harnessing
of the powerful blend of flavors so that neither sweetness nor
sourness nor bitterness dominates. Let your taste buds guide you
along your way to true cocktail enlightenment. But be warned, an
overabundance of drinking may lead to temptation from the Dark
Side, with those of weak willpower being tempted to call exes, steal
traffic cones, or become totally Sith-faced!

May the sauce be strong with you.

CONTENTS

Part I

INTRODUCTION

George Lucas's Star Wars Universe covers eleven films (with more in various stages of production), at least half a dozen television series, dozens of video games, hundreds of books and comic books, and enough merchandise to sink the Death Star.

The timeline of all these stories is rigid, vast, and at times daunting. The fourth, fifth, and sixth movies take place, chronologically, before the first, second, and third. A bold move for a relatively new filmmaker, but George Lucas wanted the audience to dive straight into the center of his epic space opera. This decision not to have a singular starting point has allowed the Star Wars franchise to become ever-expanding, growing far beyond the movies Lucas had originally planned.

The everlasting popularity of the Star Wars franchise can be attributed to amazing storytelling; the perfect balance of comedy and tragedy, moments of silliness paired with the profound. *Star Wars* is an embodiment of the stories we have been telling since the dawn of time: romance, adventure, and good versus evil. Plus, the odd space explosion (which is always a people pleaser)!

So, raise a cocktail to this space saga phenomenon and picture yourself in Mos Eisley Cantina enjoying the hot tunes.

LEVELS OF COCKTAIL ATTAINMENT

"Patience you must have, my young padawan."
—Master Yoda

All the cocktails featured in this book have been sorted into four ranks: Youngling, Padawan, Jedi Knight, and Jedi Master. Each rank indicates the level of skill, equipment, and time needed to achieve cocktail perfection.

YOUNGLING
These cocktails are simple, quick, and easy, with only a glass and ice needed! Perfect for when you just want to use what you have in the pantry.

PADAWAN
These cocktails are simple mix-and-go drinks. You do need a cocktail shaker, but these libations are great tasting and low on fuss.

JEDI KNIGHT
These cocktails need you to summon bartender's force and use special skills such as layering, rimming, and twisting, to name a few.

JEDI MASTER
These cocktails are for when you really want to show off your mastery of mixology to impress. These cocktails need special skills and tend to need some preparation beforehand. However, your patience will be rewarded with some out-of-this-galaxy cocktail creations!

BASIC EQUIPMENT

To make the perfect cocktail, you don't need to spend all your Imperial Credits on the flashiest equipment. Follow these simple bartender tricks and scavenge out a few creative solutions to make stellar cocktails from the comfort of your kitchen.

BAR SPOON
The classic bar spoon has a long, twisted handle, a flat end, and a tear-drop-shaped spoon used for measuring out and stirring spirits.

BLENDER
An electric blender is required for some recipes involving fruit and ice cubes. It doesn't need to be an expensive or powerful blender, just good enough to crush ice.

CITRUS SQUEEZER
When making delicious cocktails using fresh citrus, juice is crucial. A citrus squeezer can really save time and ensure that you get every last drop. If you don't have a squeezer, simply use your hands. Tip: To get the most juice, roll the fruit in the palm of your hands, slice it in half, and microwave for five seconds. Then, simply use a fork to squeeze the juice out.

COCKTAIL SHAKER
Coming in all different shapes and sizes, the standard shaker is stainless steel with three parts: a base known as a "can," a built-in strainer, and a cap (which can be used as a jigger). It's brilliantly straightforward and easy to keep clean. If you can't get your hands on a cocktail shaker, consider using a large glass jar with a lid and waterproof seal.

(Continued on next page)

JIGGER

The jigger is the standard measuring tool for spirits and liqueurs, and a toolbox essential for any avid cocktail maker. If you don't have a jigger, a single shot glass or even an eggcup can be a stand-in. In this book, one shot is measured as 1 oz. (30 milliliters).

MUDDLER

To extract maximum flavor from certain fresh garnishes such as mint or fruit, use a muddler to crush the ingredients. If short a muddler, a fork and some gentle poking is a good substitute.

STRAINER

Most cocktail shakers are sold with a built-in strainer. However, if yours doesn't have one, any fine mesh strainer works just as well. Tip: when a cocktail calls for straining, ensure that you've used ice cubes, as crushed ice tends to clog the strainer in standard shakers.

HOW TO

You don't need to be a Jedi Master using the Force to juggle lemons and flip bottles. The reality is much simpler and with these simple tricks anyone can become a master of mixology. To quote Master Yoda himself, "always pass on what you have learned," the lesson being to have a big party and show off your cocktail-making skills!

LAYER

Some drinks call for a careful layering of ingredients to create an ombré effect. Always start with the heaviest liquid (with the most sugar content). To add a second layer, place a spoon upside down inside the glass, but not touching the first layer of alcohol. Very slowly pour the second liquid over the back of the spoon to form a distinct second layer. Repeat for subsequent layers.

RIM

To add an extra flourish to a drink, the rim of a cocktail glass is often decorated. To achieve this, spread a few tablespoons of the desired ingredient onto a small plate. Moisten the outer rim of the glass with water, a citrus-wedge, or syrup. Then, roll the outer rim of the glass on the plate until lightly coated. Hold the glass upside down and tap to release any excess.

SHAKE

When a cocktail contains eggs, fruit juice, or cream, it is necessary to shake all the ingredients. It not only mixes the ingredients, but also chills them simultaneously. When shaking a cocktail, there is no agreement on the perfect time, but ten seconds of brisk shaking is recommended.

STIR

Using a bar spoon (or lightsaber!), stir the drink and ice gently together to chill the concoction. When condensation forms on the outside of the glass, it is ready to drink.

(Continued on next page)

TWIST

Some drinks call for a citrus twist to garnish the cocktail. This is a simple way to make a cocktail look elegant while also adding citrus notes to the aroma of the drink. Use a Y-shaped peeler or sharp paring knife to cut a thin, oval disk out of the citrus peel, avoiding the pith (the white, spongy part). Gently grasp the outer edges skin-side down between your thumb and index and middle fingers and pinch the twist over the drink. Rub the peel around the rim of the glass, then drop it into the drink.

GUIDE TO GLASSWARE

CHAMPAGNE FLUTE
This tall tulip-shaped glass is designed to show off the magical bubbles of Champagne as they burst against the glass. It's great for any cocktail made with sparkling wine.

COLLINS GLASS
These tall, narrow glasses originally got their name from the Tom Collins cocktail but are now commonly used for a vast array of mixed drinks.

COUPE GLASS
This saucer-shaped stemmed glass, rumored to have originally been designed after the shape of Marie Antoinette's breast, is traditionally used for serving champagne. However, the wide mouth is not great for containing bubbles and is now more commonly used for cocktails without ice.

GLASS GOBLET
These large tulip-shaped glasses with a short stem are designed for brandy and cognac. The large bowl shape allows for optimal air intake to bring out the flavors of the alcohol.

GLASS TANKARD (STEIN)
This traditional glass beer mug has origins leading back to medieval Germany. Perfect for serving up a drink at any castle feast.

HURRICANE GLASS
A tall, elegantly cut glass named after its hurricane lamp-like shape, it's often used for exotic/tropical drinks.

(Continued on next page)

Margarita Glass

This glass was designed with one drink in mind. The distinctive double-bowl shape works particularly well for frozen margaritas. The wide rim makes it easy to add a salt or sugar rim.

Martini Glass

As the name might suggest, this glass is designed with a particular cocktail in mind. These V-shaped long stem glasses are used for a wide range of cocktails served straight up (without ice).

Pint Glass

The pint glass is a staple of any British pub and is designed for the serving of beer and cider. This glassware is designed to hold a British imperial measurement of a pint: 20 oz./568 milliliters. Under British law, it is actually illegal to sell beer in any other glass, as consumer rights dictate that when ordering a pint of beer, it's imperative that a customer gets exactly that!

Rocks Glass

This old-fashioned glass is a short tumbler with a wide base and top, typically associated with whiskey cocktails. The glass was designed to withstand muddling and hold large cubes of ice.

Shot Glass

Used for "shooting" a drink, these small glasses are used for a straight pour of spirits.

Wine Glass

Wine glasses are not just for wine. They can also be used for wine-based cocktails such as wine spritzer.

INGREDIENTS

BUTTERFLY PEA FLOWER
Available online (we recommend b'Lure flower extract) and in certain kitchen supply stores, this relatively unknown ingredient will turn drinks from blue to purple and then pink with only a few drops! Used in traditional medicine and as a natural food coloring throughout Asia, this unique ingredient acts as a natural litmus test, changing color with the acidity of a drink.

CITRUS JUICE
Lemon, lime, or grapefruit juice can be found in the vast majority of cocktails. It is always preferable to use freshly squeezed citrus juice when making a cocktail.

EDIBLE GLITTER
Edible drink glitter is now widely available in a wide range of colors and flavors and is a great way to turn an ordinary cocktail into an extraordinary one!

EGGS
A few cocktails in this book call for egg whites and yolks. However, if you are vegan, aquafaba (the water from chickpeas) can be used as a substitute for egg whites.

FLAVORED SYRUP
Flavored syrups are a simple way to add a new twist to a cocktail. Although many are commercially available, they are also simple enough to make at home (recipes on pages 13–14).

INFUSED ALCOHOL
Flavors can easily be added to alcohols like vodka. You can really experiment with infusing using fruits and herbs, so be creative and find what tastes best to you!

(Continued on next page)

SPECIAL INGREDIENTS

Some of the recipes in this book call for some special ingredients to rec-reate alien-looking concoctions: baking soda, citric acid, sodium algi-nate, and calcium lactate. All sound as though they come straight out of a chemistry textbook, but it is important to purchase these ingredients at a high enough purity for human consumption.

HOMEMADE SYRUPS

Custom cocktail syrups are one of those special ingredients that can magically transform a drink. Whether it's basic simple syrup, a seasonal flavor combination such as vanilla syrup, or something fruity like passion fruit syrup, you can easily make it and enjoy it at home! Remember to take care and use sensible safety measures when working with heated sugar.

SIMPLE SYRUP

Sometimes referred to as sugar syrup, this simple-to-create cocktail staple is basically a supersaturated mixture of sugar and water. The most common version uses two parts sugar to one part water (2:1). To make it, add the sugar and water to a saucepan and heat at a medium temperature until all the sugar is dissolved. Then, take off the heat and allow to cool. Simple syrup can be stored for up to 1 month in the fridge.

HONEY SYRUP
- $3^{1}/_{3}$ ounces (100 milliliters) honey
- $3^{1}/_{3}$ ounces (100 milliliters) water
- *Optional:* 1 teaspoon dried lavender flowers

Honey syrup is easy to make; combine equal parts honey with water in a saucepan, heat until dissolved (no more than a minute), then cool to room temperature before using. For an extra botanical flavor, try adding some lavender flowers (see AT-AT Knees on page 64). Once cool, strain the syrup into a jar or bottle and seal tightly with a lid. Honey syrup can be stored for up to 1 month in the fridge.

(Continued on next page)

Passion Fruit Syrup

- ½ cup (100 grams) sugar
- ½ cup (130 milliliters) water
- 4 ripe passion fruits

In a small saucepan over low heat, combine the sugar and water. Stir occasionally until the sugar has completely dissolved, then remove from heat. Slice passion fruits in half and scoop out the pulp into the simple syrup. Let the fruit steep in the syrup for 2 hours. Pour the solution through a fine mesh sieve into a glass storage container with a lid. To avoid a cloudy simple syrup, don't press on the solids; let the syrup drain naturally. Store the syrup in the refrigerator for up to 1 month.

Vanilla Syrup

- ½ cup (100 grams) sugar
- ½ cup (130 milliliters) water
- 1 teaspoon vanilla extract

In a small saucepan over low heat, combine the sugar and water. Stir occasionally until the sugar has completely dissolved, then remove from heat. As the simple syrup is cooling, stir in the vanilla extract. Once cool, strain into a jar or bottle and seal tightly with a lid. Store the syrup in the refrigerator for up to 1 month.

GARNISHES

CITRUS

The most widely used garnishes are citrus fruits. Whether a cocktail calls for a citrus wheel (thin, circular cross-section), a wedge, or the more elegant twist, these garnishes don't just look fantastic, they also add aroma and flavor.

EDIBLE FLOWERS

Flowers bring a fresh botanical touch to many cocktails (as well as being picture perfect) and can be purchased online and at certain supermarkets or cake decorating supply stores. The most commonly used edible flowers in cocktail making are cornflowers, nasturtium, pansies, lavender, dandelions, and violets.

FRUIT

Many exotic cocktails call for fruit garnish such as pineapple, strawberries, or Ewoks' favorite wasaka berries, to name a few. Either cut the fruit into wedges or use a cocktail stick to skewer the fruit and lay it on top of the glass.

HERBS

Herb garnishes are often used in cocktail making. Mint is most frequently used in this book, as it not only looks pretty but adds a sweet refreshing aroma as well. To get the most out of mint, place the leaves flat between your palms and clap to really release their essential oils before placing them in your drink.

INEDIBLE FLOURISHES

A tiny cocktail umbrella, once the height of sophistication, can now look a bit outdated. But don't let this stop you from playing around with some fun space-themed flourishes. For example, try using a miniature lightsaber as a cocktail stirrer. However, in terms of the "straw wars," ditch the plastic straws in favor of reusable or eco-friendly!

Savory Garnishes

A few cocktails in this book call for savory garnishes like celery and olives. This is arguably one of the best ways to get your five-a-day.

HEALTH AND SAFETY PROTOCOL

Cocktail making is not all fun and games, so read these mandatory creeds to ensure safety reigns across the galaxy:

ACTIVATED CHARCOAL POWDER

Activated charcoal can be purchased in many health food stores. It has a long history of being used as a detoxifying agent and can dramatically change the appearance of a cocktail. However, it can be problematic if mixed with certain medication, so we recommend avoiding consuming cocktails containing charcoal if you are taking any medicine, contraceptive pills, or vitamin supplements.

DRY ICE PELLETS

Dry ice is the common name for solid carbon dioxide. It is appearing in more and more cocktails and can be ordered relatively easily online, but dry ice does not stay solid forever, so timing is key.

Dry ice begins to sublimate at -108°F (-78°C), therefore care must be taken when handling. Gloves should always be worn when handling dry ice to make sure that there is no contact with bare skin. It is also essential to only use dry ice in a well-ventilated area.

For cocktail making, dry ice pellets work best, as this allows you to only add as needed (typically 2–3 pellets per cocktail). The pellets will quickly dissolve to create a smoky/foggy effect. Take care when adding dry ice pellets to a drink; the drink will often fizz over if you add too many too quickly.

Most important, *never* consume a dry ice pellet, as this can lead to some serious health problems. Always wait for the smoky/foggy effect to finish before taking your first sip.

SPARKLERS

To add an extra "wow" factor to your cocktails, try indoor mini sparklers. Always light away from flammable material and wait until the sparkler is fully extinguished before taking a sip! Be prepared to watch the sparks fly and impress your friends.

Part II
COCKTAILS

LIGHT SIDE

Baby Yo-daiquiri

Arguably the most adorable cocktail in the galaxy! No one will be able to resist sampling this sweet and refreshing fruit daiquiri. However, don't let looks deceive you. Although small, the Force is strong in the Baby Yo-daiquiri with a powerful blend of melon liqueur and light rum.

COCKTAIL DIFFICULTY: JEDI KNIGHT
SERVES: 1
PREPARATION TIME: 5 MINUTES
GLASSWARE: COUPE GLASS

1 ounce (30 milliliters) light rum
1 ounce (30 milliliters) melon liqueur
1 ounce (30 milliliters) fresh lime juice
ice cubes
Garnishes: 1 burlap napkin, 2 blueberries, 1 cocktail stick, and 2 lime slices

/ First, tie the burlap napkin around a coupe glass to form the robe of the Baby Yo-daiquiri.

/ Next, add the 2 blueberries on the cocktail stick for eyes and 2 lime slices for ears.

/ For the cocktail, combine the rum, melon liqueur, and lime juice in a cocktail shaker along with a handful of ice cubes. Shake until cool and strain into the decorated coupe glass.

Drink It, You Must!

Learn from the Jedi Master himself and use the Force to create this wonderful levitating Yoda soda float. Once you add the ice cream, it will fizz and create a swampy green foam just like the many lagoons of Dagobah. However, instead of bogwings, dragonsnakes, and swamp slugs, the only surprise hiding beneath this foaming surface is a delicious and refreshing cocktail. Drink it, you must!

COCKTAIL DIFFICULTY: YOUNGLING
SERVES: 1
PREPARATION TIME: 5 MINUTES
GLASSWARE: HURRICANE

2 ounces (60 milliliters) gin
4 ounces (120 milliliters) tonic water, chilled
½ ounce (15 milliliters) fresh lime juice
1 teaspoon green food coloring
Scoop vanilla ice cream
Garnish: 1 lime wheel

/ Combine the gin, chilled tonic water, fresh lime juice, and green food coloring in a hurricane glass. Use a bar spoon to gently mix the ingredients together.

/ Add a scoop of vanilla ice cream and garnish with a lime wheel before serving.

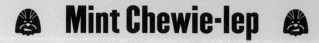

Mint Chewie-lep

Just like Chewbacca's tree-covered home planet of Kashyyyk, this cocktail has an abundance of thick green vegetation, with a strong combination of aromatic bitters and oaky bourbon flavors hiding among the mint leaves.

COCKTAIL DIFFICULTY: PADAWAN
SERVES: 1
PREPARATION TIME: 5 MINUTES
GLASSWARE: COPPER MUG

8 mint leaves
½ ounce (15 milliliters) simple syrup (see recipe on page 13)
2½ ounces (75 milliliters) bourbon whiskey
crushed ice
Garnishes: mint sprig and 3 drops angostura bitters

/ In a copper mug, lightly muddle the mint leaves in the simple syrup.

/ Add in the bourbon whiskey, then pack the glass tightly with crushed ice. Stir until the cup is frosted on the outside.

/ Top with crushed ice to form an ice dome and garnish with a mint sprig and angostura bitters.

The Kessel Rum

Whether you are drinking solo or with your crew, this record-breaking cocktail is a favorite among smugglers, scavengers, and wrongdoers alike. With sweet golden spiced rum straight from the spice mines of Kessel, let this tropical cocktail transport you into hyperspace in under 12 parsecs!

COCKTAIL DIFFICULTY: JEDI KNIGHT
SERVES: 1
PREPARATION TIME: 5 MINUTES
GLASSWARE: GLASS TANKARD

2 ounces (60 milliliters) golden spiced rum

½ ounce (15 milliliters) coconut rum

2 ounces (60 milliliters) pineapple juice

½ ounce (15 milliliters) passion fruit syrup (recipe on page 14)

½ ounce (15 milliliters) fresh lime juice

ice cubes

crushed ice

Garnish: pineapple wedge

/ Combine the rums, pineapple juice, passion fruit syrup, and fresh lime juice in a cocktail shaker along with a handful of ice cubes. Shake vigorously until the contents are cool.

/ Strain into a glass tankard over crushed ice and garnish with a pineapple wedge.

Rye-Walker Sour

The Rye–Walker Sour is the perfect cocktail to get through any awkward family reunion. Whether your father is the Dark Sith Lord who has been trying to kill you or you accidentally locked lips with the secret twin sister you never knew about, all of life's problems will simply melt away into the cosmos with this deliciously devious cocktail!

COCKTAIL DIFFICULTY: JEDI KNIGHT
SERVES: 1
PREPARATION TIME: 5 MINUTES
GLASSWARE: ROCKS GLASS

2 ounces (60 milliliters) rye whiskey

1 ounce (30 milliliters) fresh lemon juice

½ ounce (15 milliliters) simple syrup (recipe on page 13)

2 dashes (2 milliliters) angostura bitters

½ fresh egg white

ice cubes

crushed ice

Garnish: 1 orange wedge and 1 cherry

/ Combine the rye whiskey, fresh lemon juice, simple syrup, angostura bitters, and egg white in a cocktail shaker with a handful of ice cubes and shake until chilled.

/ Strain over crushed ice in a rocks glass. Garnish with an orange wedge and a cherry.

Qui-Gon Gin Sling

Discovering this drink is the will of the Force, and one you will be handsomely rewarded for. Based on the classic Gin Sling, the Qui-Gon Gin Sling is the perfect balance of sweet, sour, bitter, and herbal flavors, so become one with this drink and let it aid you on your path to enlightenment (or at least to a great night out).

COCKTAIL DIFFICULTY: PADAWAN
SERVES: 1
PREPARATION TIME: 5 MINUTES
GLASSWARE: COLLINS GLASS

1½ ounces (45 milliliters) gin
1 ounce (30 milliliters) sweet vermouth
1 ounce (30 milliliters) simple syrup (recipe on page 13)
¾ ounce (22 milliliters) fresh lemon juice
1 dash (1 milliliter) angostura bitters
ice cubes
club soda, to top glass
Garnish: 1 lemon spiral

/ Combine the gin, sweet vermouth, simple syrup, fresh lemon juice, and angostura bitters into a cocktail shaker with a handful of ice cubes. Shake until cool.

/ Strain the cocktail into a Collins glass filled with ice cubes and top with club soda. Garnish with a lemon spiral before serving.

The Princess's Golden Bellini

This cocktail takes its inspiration from that infamous golden bikini worn by Leia which awakened the Force for many a teenager across the galaxy! With peaches and bubbly making it both sweet and luxurious, this golden delight is perfectly fit for a princess.

COCKTAIL DIFFICULTY: JEDI KNIGHT
SERVES: 1
PREPARATION TIME: 10 MINUTES
GLASSWARE: CHAMPAGNE FLUTE

For the Peach Puree
4 medium white peaches, pitted and quartered
3 ice cubes
1 teaspoon fresh lemon juice
¾ ounces (22 milliliters) simple syrup (recipe on page 13)

For the Cocktail
2 ounces (60 milliliters) peach puree
prosecco, to top glass
pinch golden edible glitter
Garnish: 1 peach slice

/ For the peach puree, to a blender add the peaches, ice cubes, lemon juice and simple syrup and blend until smooth.

/ Next, pour the peach puree into a champagne flute and top with prosecco.

/ Add a pinch of golden edible glitter for an extra touch and gently stir with a bar spoon to bring the drink together.

/ Garnish with a peach slice before serving.

Wookiee Woo Woo

It is a well-regarded fact across the galaxy that for any party to truly be legendary you need a Wookiee to be involved! Therefore, I've taken inspiration from these furry, fuzzy party animals to create the Wookiee Woo Woo. This fun and fruity drink will get your guests crying out "RAWRGWAWGGR" in delight!

COCKTAIL DIFFICULTY: YOUNGLING
SERVES: 1
PREPARATION TIME: 5 MINUTES
GLASSWARE: MARTINI GLASS

1 ounce (30 milliliters) vodka

1 ounce (30 milliliters) peach schnapps

few drops fresh lime juice

2 ounces (60 milliliters) cranberry juice

ice cubes

Garnish: 1 flared lime wheel (to create your very own fuzzball)

/ Combine the vodka, schnapps, lime juice, and cranberry juice in a cocktail shaker half-filled with ice cubes. Shake until cool, then strain into a martini glass.

/ Garnish with a flared lime wheel before serving.

Mando Commando Cocktail

The recipe for this cocktail (based on the classic Negroni) has been passed down from generation to generation of Mandalorians. Once feared to be nearly wiped out, the Mando Commando Cocktail is coming back to popularity with a mighty vengeance. Follow these simple creeds, as "this is the way" to make a great drink!

COCKTAIL DIFFICULTY: YOUNGLING
SERVES: 1
PREPARATION TIME: 5 MINUTES
GLASSWARE: ROCKS GLASS

ice cubes

1 ounce (30 milliliters) gin

1 ounce (30 milliliters) Campari

1 ounce (30 milliliters) sweet vermouth

1 large novelty cube (the bigger the better)

Garnish: 1 citrus twist

/ Combine the ice cubes, gin, Campari, and sweet vermouth into the base of a cocktail shaker. Using a bar spoon, stir well until the glass feels cold to the touch.

/ Add a large novelty ice cube to a rocks glass and strain in the ingredients from the cocktail shaker.

/ Garnish with a citrus twist.

Droid's Mind Eraser

This seriously potent cocktail is guaranteed to get you fully charged up and ready to bust out your best C-3PO moves on the dance floor. And with its strong blend of coffee liqueur and vodka, this drink works as well as Babu Frik's memory wipe to help you forget all those cringeworthy memories from the night before!

COCKTAIL DIFFICULTY: YOUNGLING
SERVES: 1
PREPARATION TIME: 5 MINUTES
GLASSWARE: COUPE GLASS

2 ounces (60 milliliters)
    coffee liqueur
2 ounces (60 milliliters)
    vodka
ice cubes
club soda, to top glass

/ Combine the coffee liqueur and vodka in an ice-filled glass.

/ Top up with club soda and serve.

Obi-Wine Kenobi

Say "Hello there" to the Obi-Wine Kenobi! A fantastic summer cocktail with both sweet and citrus flavors, this is the perfect drink to drown any Grievous and get you planning your next epic adventure like a true Jedi Master.

COCKTAIL DIFFICULTY: PADAWAN
SERVES: 6-8
PREPARATION TIME: 10 MINUTES
GLASSWARE: 1 PITCHER AND 6-8 MASON JARS

2 lemons (cut into thin slices)

2 limes (cut into thin slices)

1 orange (cut into thin slices)

several mint leaves, roughly torn

6 ounces (180 milliliters) agave nectar

5 ounces (150 milliliters) light tequila

2 ounces (60 milliliters) fresh lime juice

1 bottle red wine

club soda, to top glass

Garnish: mint leaves, torn

/ Combine the sliced fruit, mint leaves, agave nectar, tequila, lime juice, and red wine in a large pitcher.

/ Give the mixture a vigorous stir and top with club soda. Allow the cocktail to chill in the fridge for at least an hour before serving.

/ To serve, pour the cocktail into mason jars and garnish with torn mint leaves.

Republic's Old Fashioned

The Old Republic was a time of many a Jedi, many a Sith, and many a reason to drink! Enjoy sipping this cocktail classic while you plan for the many battles ahead.

COCKTAIL DIFFICULTY: YOUNGLING
SERVES: 1
PREPARATION TIME: 5 MINUTES
GLASSWARE: ROCKS GLASS

¼ ounce (7.5 milliliters) simple syrup (see recipe on page 13)

½ teaspoon angostura bitters

1 teaspoon water

1 ice cube

2 ounces (60 milliliters) bourbon whiskey

Garnish: 1 orange peel

/ Combine the simple syrup, bitters, and water in a rocks glass. Add an ice cube and stir in the bourbon.

/ Garnish with an orange peel.

Finn Fizz

Based on the classic Gin Fizz, the Finn Fizz is always ready to save the day (just like its namesake). Therefore, when you need to rescue a party, you won't find a more popular savior than this!

COCKTAIL DIFFICULTY: YOUNGLING
SERVES: 1
PREPARATION TIME: 5 MINUTES
GLASSWARE: COLLINS GLASS

1½ ounces (45 milliliters) gin
1 ounce (30 milliliters) fresh lemon juice
1 egg white
2 tablespoons simple syrup (recipe on page 13)
ice cubes
sparkling water, to top glass
Garnish: 1 lemon slice

/ Combine the gin, fresh lemon juice, egg white, and simple syrup into a cocktail shaker along with a handful of ice cubes. Shake until cold and strain into a Collins glass filled with ice cubes.

/ Top with sparkling water and garnish with a lemon slice before serving.

DARK SIDE

Dark 'N' Stormy Side

Give in to the Dark 'N' Stormy Side with this tantalizing dark rum cocktail. As Master Yoda himself said, "once you start down the dark path, forever will it dominate your destiny," so embrace the dark side and enjoy the power of finding your new favorite cocktail.

COCKTAIL DIFFICULTY: YOUNGLING
SERVES: 1
PREPARATION TIME: 5 MINUTES
GLASSWARE: COLLINS GLASS

ice cubes

1¾ ounces (50 milliliters)
dark rum

½ ounce (15 milliliters)
fresh lime juice

¼ ounce (7.5 milliliters)
simple syrup (see recipe
on page 13)

chilled ginger beer, to top
glass

Garnish: 1 lime wedge

/ Fill a Collins glass with a handful
of ice and combine the rum,
lime juice, and simple syrup.

/ Top with ginger beer and stir
gently. Garnish with a wedge of
lime.

Diki-Diki-Dooku

While first appearing sweet and refreshing, this cocktail has a dark side and can deliver a decapitating hangover the next day. But don't be dismayed, as those who are at one with the Force will not be led astray.

COCKTAIL DIFFICULTY: PADAWAN
SERVES: 1
PREPARATION TIME: 5 MINUTES
GLASSWARE: MARTINI GLASS

2 ounces (60 milliliters) gin
1 ounce (30 milliliters) pink
  grapefruit juice
1 ounce (30 milliliters)
  Swedish Punsch
ice cubes

/ Combine the gin, grapefruit juice, and Swedish Punsch into a cocktail shaker with a handful of ice cubes. Shake until cool and strain into a martini glass.

Darth Mauled Cider

This winning winter warming cocktail is enough to put a smile on anyone's red and heavily tattooed face, but be careful not to overindulge this festive season, as you don't want to end up sith-faced with a splitting headache in the morning.

COCKTAIL DIFFICULTY: JEDI MASTER
SERVES: 8
PREPARATION TIME: 20 MINUTES
GLASSWARE: GOBLET GLASS

25 ounces (750 milliliters) dry cider
3 tablespoons brandy
8.5 ounces (250 milliliters) apple juice
1 strip lemon peel
1 lemon zest
1 orange (zest and slices)
½ teaspoon nutmeg
3 whole cloves
1 cinnamon stick
1 thumb-size piece fresh ginger, sliced
Garnish: 1 cinnamon stick

/ Pour the dry cider into a saucepan and add the brandy, apple juice, lemon peel, lemon zest, orange zest and slices, nutmeg, cloves, cinnamon stick, and ginger.

/ Gently simmer for 5 to 10 minutes, then remove the lemon peel, orange slices, whole spices, and ginger using tongs or strain through a sieve before serving.

/ Garnish with a stick of cinnamon.

Emperor Palpatini

The Emperor Palpatini is the perfect drink to lord over others. The darkest known cocktail in the galaxy, thanks to a sprinkling of activated charcoal, it is alluring with its mesmerizing looks and insidious alcohol contents.

COCKTAIL DIFFICULTY: JEDI KNIGHT
SERVES: 1
PREPARATION TIME: 5 MINUTES
GLASSWARE: COUPE GLASS

1½ ounces (45 milliliters) light rum

¼ teaspoon activated charcoal*

½ ounce (15 milliliters) fresh lemon juice

½ ounce (15 milliliters) fresh lime juice

1 ounce (30 milliliters) simple syrup (see recipe on page 13)

¼ ounce (5 milliliters) maraschino liqueur

ice cubes

Garnish: dry ice pellets**

/ Combine the rum, activated charcoal, juices, simple syrup, and maraschino liqueur into a cocktail shaker along with a handful of ice cubes.

/ Shake until cold and strain into a coupe glass. Add some dry ice to give it an extra evil effect.

---

*See guidance on activated charcoal powder in Health and Safety Protocol on page 17.
**See guidance on dry ice pellets in Health and Safety Protocol on page 17.

Death Star Martini

The Death Star Martini is the Empire's ultimate cocktail. Arm yourself with a few of these cocktails and you will be guaranteed to destroy it on the dance floor!

COCKTAIL DIFFICULTY: JEDI KNIGHT
SERVES: 2
PREPARATION TIME: 5 MINUTES
GLASSWARE: MARTINI GLASS

2 ripe passion fruits
2 ounces (60 milliliters) vanilla vodka
I ounce (30 milliliters) passion fruit liqueur
I tablespoon fresh lime juice
I tablespoon simple syrup (see recipe on page 13)
ice cubes
prosecco, to top glass
Garnish: I dried passion fruit wheel

/ Scoop the seeds from the passion fruits into the bottom of a cocktail shaker.

/ Next, add the vodka, passion fruit liqueur, lime juice and simple syrup.

/ Combine with a handful of ice cubes and shake vigorously until the mixture is cool.

/ Strain into two martini glasses and top with prosecco.

/ Garnish with a dried passion fruit wheel.

Mango Jango Sour

This cocktail may appear to be difficult to prepare but no need to Boba fret. Once you have learned the ways of mixology you will be able to clone up a whole troop of these refreshing fruity treats!

COCKTAIL DIFFICULTY: JEDI MASTER
SERVES: 4
PREPARATION TIME: 30 MINUTES
GLASSWARE: TUMBLER

10½ ounces (300 grams) mango, chopped

3½ ounces (100 grams) granulated sugar

1 thin slice fresh ginger

3⅓ ounces (100 milliliters) water

1½ ounces (45 milliliters) fresh lime juice

7 ounces (200 milliliters) Pisco

1 egg white

ice cubes

Garnish: few drops angostura bitters

/ Place the mango, granulated sugar, and ginger into a medium-sized saucepan and add the water.

/ Stir and bring to a simmer for 7 to 8 minutes or until the mango has started to soften. Take off the heat and let cool for 10 to 15 minutes.

/ Pour the cooled mango syrup through a sieve into a cocktail shaker.

/ Next, combine the lime juice, Pisco, and egg white into the cocktail shaker along with a few handfuls of ice cubes. Shake until cold and strain into a tumbler.

/ Add a few drops of angostura bitters to the top of each cocktail before serving.

Kylo Rye

Enjoy this brooding sour cocktail of aromatic rye whiskey and angostura bitters. The perfect drink to get you through any teenage angst and help you plot your next move to rule the galaxy.

COCKTAIL DIFFICULTY: PADAWAN
SERVES: 1
PREPARATION TIME: 5 MINUTES
GLASSWARE: MARTINI GLASS

2 ounces (60 milliliters) rye whiskey

¾ ounce (25 milliliters) rosso vermouth

½ ounce syrup from a jar of maraschino cherries

2 dashes angostura bitters

ice cubes

Garnish: 1 cherry and 1 lemon twist

/ Combine the whiskey, rosso vermouth, syrup, and bitters in a cocktail shaker with a handful of ice cubes.

/ Shake until cool, then strain into a martini glass and garnish with a cherry and a twist of lemon.

Stormtrooper Shooters

Have a blast serving up a squad of these fun and guilt-free dessert shooters. Unlike their namesake, these shooters won't miss their mark!

COCKTAIL DIFFICULTY: PADAWAN
SERVES: 1
PREPARATION TIME: 5 MINUTES
GLASSWARE: SHOT GLASS

½ ounce (15 milliliters) almond liqueur

½ ounce (15 milliliters) coffee liqueur

½ ounce (15 milliliters) double cream

Garnish: whipped cream

/ Pour the almond and coffee liqueur into a shot glass.

/ Layer the double cream on top by slowly pouring it over a spoon touching the side of the shot glass. Garnish with whipped cream.

Mai TIE Fighter

While sipping one of these tropical cocktails you will be able to maneuver any party situation thrown your way. Get light-years ahead of your Star Wars–themed party by creating the iconic symbol of the Imperial fleet as the perfect garnish for this stellar little cocktail.

COCKTAIL DIFFICULTY: JEDI KNIGHT
SERVES: 1
PREPARATION TIME: 5 MINUTES
GLASSWARE: COLLINS GLASS

½ ounce (45 milliliters) light rum

½ ounce (15 milliliters) dark rum

½ ounce (15 milliliters) orgeat

¾ ounce (22.5 milliliters) orange curaçao

1 ounce (30 milliliters) fresh lime juice

ice cubes

1 teaspoon grenadine

Garnish: 1 grape pierced with 2 cocktail sticks and two hexagonally cut pineapple slices

/ Combine the rums, orgeat, orange curaçao, and lime juice in a cocktail shaker with a handful of ice cubes. Shake until the mixture is cool.

/ Strain into a Collins glass filled with ice cubes.

/ Create an ombre effect by slowly pouring in the grenadine using the side of the glass and the back of a spoon.

/ Garnish with a mini TIE Fighter made up of a grape pierced with 2 cocktail sticks and bookended with 2 hexagonally cut pineapple slices.

CANTINA CLASSICS

Jedi Mind Trick

These are the cocktails you are looking for! Every cocktail padawan needs to master making the Jedi Mind Trick! Be warned, however, that this little cocktail can be very suggestive, and drinkers may find themselves doing things they would have never expected. Well, after two or three of them anyway . . .

COCKTAIL DIFFICULTY: YOUNGLING
SERVES: 1
PREPARATION TIME: 5 MINUTES
GLASSWARE: MARTINI GLASS

2 ounces (60 milliliters)
  vodka
½ ounce (15 milliliters) dry
  vermouth
ice cubes
Garnish: 1 lemon twist and
  1 cocktail stirrer (or
  miniature lightsaber)

Combine the vodka and dry vermouth in a cocktail shaker with a handful of ice cubes. Shake until cool, then strain into a martini glass and garnish with a lemon twist and stirrer of choice.

Mos Eisley Cantina Margarita

With hot tunes, shady figures, and the occasional outbreak of shocking violence, Mos Eisley Cantina is the must visit location for any travelers with some down time when visiting Tatooine. The first drink to try is the Mos Eisley Cantina Margarita; the perfect blend of sweet dragon fruit and powerful tequila. So, enjoy a sip and listen to the swing band play.

COCKTAIL DIFFICULTY: JEDI KNIGHT
SERVES: 2
PREPARATION TIME: 5 MINUTES
GLASSWARE: MARGARITA GLASSES

1 drop green food coloring, to rim glass

1 tablespoon salt

1 dragon fruit

2 ounces (60 milliliters) fresh lime juice

1½ ounces (45 milliliters) honey syrup (see recipe on page 13)

3 ounces (90 milliliters) tequila

ice cubes

/ Combine green food coloring and salt together in a mortar and pestle and rim the glasses (learn how to rim a glass on page 7).

/ Halve the dragon fruit and scoop out the flesh with a spoon. Next, combine the dragon fruit with the lime juice, honey syrup, tequila, and ice in a blender and blend until smooth.

/ Serve in the prepared salt-rimmed glasses.

Blue Bantha Milkshake

One of the most popular drinks available in the Outer Rim and a personal favorite of Luke Skywalker, this eye-catching blue cocktail is good enough for queens, farmers, and everyone in between!

COCKTAIL DIFFICULTY: PADAWAN
SERVES: 1
PREPARATION TIME: 5 MINUTES
GLASSWARE: HURRICANE GLASS

ice cubes

2 ounces (60 milliliters) blue curaçao

1 ounce (30 milliliters) coconut rum

1 ounce (30 milliliters) almond liqueur

½ ounce (15 milliliters) orgeat syrup

½ ounce (15 milliliters) vanilla syrup (see recipe on page 14)

2 ounces (60 milliliters) milk

1 ounce (30 milliliters) single cream

Garnish: sprinkle freshly ground nutmeg

/ Combine all ingredients in a blender and blend until smooth.

/ Pour into a hurricane glass and garnish with a sprinkle of freshly ground nutmeg.

 Spotchka

Spotchka was the drink of choice for Din Djarin as well as elite assassin Fennec Shand. Originally derived for a krill farmed on the planet Sorgan, this bioluminescent beverage is a must-try. Wow guests by using a black light to show off this glow-in-the-dark delight!

COCKTAIL DIFFICULTY: PADAWAN
SERVES: 1
PREPARATION TIME: 5 MINUTES
GLASSWARE: COLLINS GLASS

several dry ice pellets*
2 ounces (60 milliliters)
  botanical gin
1 ounce (30 milliliters) blue
  curaçao
tonic water, to top glass

/ Add several pellets of dry ice to a Collins glass and carefully pour over the gin, blue curaçao, and tonic water.

/ Serve this drink to guests under a black light to get the full effect of this alien drink.

*See guidance on dry ice pellets in Health and Safety Protocol on page 17.

Jabba's Jungle Juice

A seriously strong cocktail resulting from the combination of three powerful spirits: vodka, triple sec, and rum. So cut loose and show off your best karaoke, because if you choke you can always blame it on Jabba's Jungle Juice.

COCKTAIL DIFFICULTY: PADAWAN
SERVES: 1
PREPARATION TIME: 10 MINUTES
GLASSWARE: COLLINS GLASS

ice cubes

1½ ounces (45 milliliters) vodka

1 ounce (30 milliliters) fresh lime juice

1½ ounces (45 milliliters) pineapple juice

¾ ounce (22.5 milliliters) triple sec

1½ ounces (45 milliliters) orange juice

1½ ounces (45 milliliters) cranberry juice

1½ ounces (45 milliliters) light rum

½ ounce (15 milliliters) simple syrup (see recipe on page 13)

Garnish: 1 lime slice and 1 orange slice

/ Combine all ingredients in a shaker. Shake until cool and strain into a Collins glass.

/ Garnish with lime and orange slices.

AT-AT Knees

This reboot on the classic Bee's Knees cocktail will transport you to a galaxy far, far away. But beware, a few of these may make your knees tremble, especially if you're in your party shoes!

COCKTAIL DIFFICULTY: JEDI KNIGHT
SERVES: 1
PREPARATION TIME: 5 MINUTES
GLASSWARE: COUPE GLASS

2 ounces (60 milliliters) gin
¾ ounce (25 milliliters)
  honey lavender syrup
  (recipe on page 13)
¾ ounce (25 milliliters)
  fresh lemon juice
pinch edible glitter
ice cubes
Garnish: 1 lavender sprig and
  1 piece honeycomb

/ Combine the gin, honey lavender syrup, lemon juice, and edible glitter into a cocktail shaker with a handful of ice cubes. Shake until cool and strain into a coupe glass.

/ Garnish with a lavender sprig and a piece of honeycomb.

Jet Fuel

This classic coffee cocktail allows you to refuel and reenergize so that you can party from dusk to dawn. Prepare to blast off, as this version of Jet Fuel tastes out of this world!

COCKTAIL DIFFICULTY: JEDI MASTER
SERVES: 1
PREPARATION TIME: 5 MINUTES
GLASSWARE: MARTINI GLASS

2 ounces (60 milliliters) vodka

1¾ ounces (50 milliliters) coffee liqueur

1¾ ounces (50 milliliters) chilled espresso

ice cubes

Garnish: 2–3 coffee beans

/ Combine the vodka, coffee liqueur, and espresso in a shaker with a handful of ice cubes. Shake until cool and strain into a martini glass.

/ Garnish with 2 to 3 coffee beans.

Carbon Freeze

The Carbon Freeze bubbles and smokes, so be sure to strike a pose with this picture-perfect drink at your next Star Wars-themed party.

COCKTAIL DIFFICULTY: PADAWAN
SERVES: 1
PREPARATION TIME: 5 MINUTES
GLASSWARE: COLLINS GLASS

ice cubes
2 ounces (60 milliliters)
   whiskey
½ ounce (15 milliliters)
   fresh lemon juice
sparkling water, to top glass
Garnish: 1 lemon wheel and
   dry ice pellets*

/ Fill a Collins glass with ice, add the whiskey and lemon juice, and top with sparkling water.

/ Garnish with a lemon wheel and several pellets of dry ice to really impress.

*See guidance on dry ice pellets in Health and Safety Protocol on page 17.

Canto Bight Casino

Canto Bight is the playground of the most glamorous beings in the galaxy with big money card games, high stakes fathier races, and some of the fanciest cocktails outside of Coruscant—the Canto Bight Casino being one of the best! Take a gamble on this luxurious elixir and we can guarantee you won't be a loser.

COCKTAIL DIFFICULTY: JEDI KNIGHT
SERVES: 1
PREPARATION TIME: 5 MINUTES
GLASSWARE: COUPE GLASS

4 ounces (120 milliliters) gin
¼ ounce (7.5 milliliters) maraschino liqueur
¼ ounce (7.5 milliliters) fresh lemon juice
4 dashes orange bitters
ice cubes
Garnish: 1 maraschino cherry and chocolate gold coins

/ Combine the gin, maraschino liqueur, lemon juice, and orange bitters in a cocktail shaker with a handful of ice cubes.

/ Shake until cool, then strain into a coupe glass. Garnish with a maraschino cherry and scatter some chocolate gold coins around the glass to really show off your wealth to guests.

Force Dyad

This truly eye-catching cocktail serves as the perfect accompaniment to any bonding session with an old friend, so let the distance between you fade as the healing force works its wonders.

COCKTAIL DIFFICULTY: JEDI KNIGHT
SERVES: 1
PREPARATION TIME: 5 MINUTES
GLASSWARE: COLLINS GLASS

1 ounce (30 milliliters) vodka

1 ounce (30 milliliters) gin

1½ ounces (45 milliliters) grenadine

ice cubes

novelty LED ice cubes

lemonade, to top glass

1 ounce (30 milliliters) blue curaçao

/ Combine the vodka, gin, and grenadine in a cocktail shaker with a handful of ice cubes. Shake until the mixture is cool.

/ Pour into the base of a Collins glass and add the LED ice cubes.

/ Carefully pour in the lemonade using the back of a spoon, taking care not to disturb the grenadine layer, and fill the glass ¾ full.

/ Layer the blue curaçao using the back of a spoon to achieve distinct colored layers (learn how to layer a cocktail on page 7).

Kyber Sugar Crystal Cocktail

Lightsabers aren't the only powerful weapon powered by kyber cystals! Allow guests to pick their color of choice before partying through the sugar high from these sweet treats.

COCKTAIL DIFFICULTY: JEDI MASTER
SERVES: 1
PREPARATION TIME: 5 MINUTES
GLASSWARE: CHAMPAGNE FLUTE

I ounce (30 milliliters)
   vodka
½ ounce (15 milliliters)
   fresh lime juice
½ ounce (15 milliliters)
   elderflower liqueur
ice cubes
champagne, to top glass
Garnish: Rock Candy Sticks
   (recipe on page 74)

/ Combine the vodka, lime juice, and elderflower liqueur in a cocktail shaker with a handful of ice cubes. Shake until cool, then strain into a champagne flute.

/ Top with champagne and garnish with a rock candy stick.

Rock Candy Sticks

SERVES: 12

4 glass mason/jam jars
4 wooden skewers or pieces
  string
4 clothespins
12 cocktail sticks
1 cup (250 milliliters) water
3 cups (135 grams)
  granulated sugar
3–5 drops food coloring in
  classic lightsaber colors
4 sheets plastic wrap

/ Clean the glass jars thoroughly with hot water. Add a wooden skewer or string that hangs about 1 inch from the bottom of each jar. Balance clothespins across the tops of the jars to hold the skewers or strings in place.

/ Wet each cocktail stick with water and roll it in granulated sugar. (This gives the sugar crystals a base layer to start from.) Set these aside to dry while you prepare the sugar syrup.

/ Place the water in a medium-sized pan and bring it to a boil. Slowly add in the sugar and stir. Continue to stir and boil the syrup until all the sugar has completely dissolved. Remove pan from heat and allow the sugar syrup to cool for 20 to 30 minutes.

/ Pour the cooled solution into the prepared jars. Add 3 to 5 drops of food coloring to each jar. Lower one sugared cocktail stick into each jar until it hangs 1 inch from the bottom. Carefully place your jar in a cool place, away from harsh light, where it can sit undisturbed. Cover the top loosely with plastic wrap.

/ You should start to see sugar crystals forming within 2 to 4 hours. If you see no change after 24 hours, dissolve some more sugar in the solution. Allow the rock candy to grow (approximately 3 to 6 days) until it is the size you want.

/ Transfer the rock candy to an empty jar or glass (keep the clothespins to balance it) and allow it to dry for 1 to 2 hours, then serve and enjoy immediately or wrap in plastic wrap to save for later (up to 6 months).

CREATURE CREATIONS

Bacta Tank

Grogu was not able to resist these delicious floating pearls and neither will your guests as you amaze them with this strange creation. Watch the Aperol-infused pearls float around in your glass before bursting in your mouth to release their tasty rhubarb and orange flavors.

COCKTAIL DIFFICULTY: JEDI MASTER
SERVES: 8+
PREPARATION TIME: 30-45 MINUTES
GLASSWARE: COLLINS GLASS

For the Aperol Pearls

3½ ounces (100 milliliters) Aperol

1 teaspoon orange food coloring

1 gram food-grade sodium alginate made from seaweed extracts

1 bottled water (if calcium content of tap water is too high, the reverse spherification won't work)

1 gram food-grade calcium lactate

1 pipette

For the Cocktail (per serving)

1 ounce (30 milliliters) vodka

1 ounce (30 milliliters) blue curaçao

lemonade, to top glass

/ To make the Aperol pearls, in a bowl combine the Aperol and orange food coloring with the sodium alginate and mix together with a whisk or fork. This process can take 10 to 15 minutes, as the sodium alginate can take some time to fully dissolve. Once dissolved, set aside until most of the bubbles are gone; this should result in a thick mixture.

/ Next, fill a shallow baking tray with bottled water and dissolve the calcium lactate by gently stirring. Fill a pipette with the Aperol mixture and carefully allow single drops to fall into the water from a height of approximately 6 inches above the water's surface. The mixture should immediately solidify when it hits the water's surface, forming solid spheres with liquid centers.

(Continued on next page)

/ Continue this process until the desired number of spheres has been achieved, then carefully fish them out with a fork or small sieve and place them in a jar or resealable Tupperware. Once all the spheres are formed, gently place them in a sieve and wash with water, then add them to a jar or Tupperware submerged with Aperol until required. The cocktail bubbles can be stored in the refrigerator for up to 1 month.

/ To make the cocktail, place several pearls in a Collins glass, add the vodka and blue curaçao, and top with lemonade. The spheres should float up and down the glass to create a lava lamp effect before settling at the surface.

Long-Necked Kaminoan Iced Tea

This perfectly engineered extragalactic cocktail is the combination of five strong spirits all served up in one elegantly elongated glass.

COCKTAIL DIFFICULTY: PADAWAN
SERVES: 1
PREPARATION TIME: 10 MINUTES
GLASSWARE: COLLINS GLASS

½ ounce (15 milliliters) light rum

½ ounce (15 milliliters) gin

½ ounce (15 milliliters) vodka

½ ounce (15 milliliters) light tequila

½ ounce (15 milliliters) triple sec

½ ounce (15 milliliters) simple syrup (see recipe on page 13)

½ ounce (15 milliliters) fresh lemon juice

½ ounce (15 milliliters) fresh lime juice

ice cubes

cola, to top the glass

Garnish: 1 sprig mint and 1 lemon wheel

/ Combine the alcohols, triple sec, syrup, and juices in a cocktail shaker with a handful of ice cubes. Shake until cool, then strain into a Collins glass and top with cola.

/ Garnish with a mint sprig and a lemon wheel.

Jawa's Utini Martini

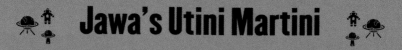

Scavenge up the ingredients for this scrumptious martini! Perfect for planning those hot summer getaways to even hotter desert planets.

COCKTAIL DIFFICULTY: JEDI KNIGHT
SERVES: 1
PREPARATION TIME: 5 MINUTES
GLASSWARE: MARTINI GLASS

I tablespoon white granulated sugar

zest of ½ lemon

1½ ounces (45 milliliters) vodka

¾ ounce (25 milliliters) triple sec

¾ ounce (25 milliliters) fresh lemon juice

ice cubes

pinch edible glitter

/ Mix the sugar with the lemon zest. Next, rim a martini glass with the sugar and lemon zest mix (learn how to rim a glass on page 7).

/ In a cocktail shaker, combine the vodka, triple sec, and lemon juice in a cocktail shaker half-filled with ice cubes. Shake until cool, then strain into the sugar-rimmed martini glass. Add a pinch of edible glitter for an extra splash of celebration.

Fuzzy Ewok

This Star Wars reboot of the classic Fuzzy Navel is all the wilder. But, like Ewoks themselves, don't let this cute cocktail fool you—it can turn its drinkers into real party animals. Perfect to serve at any celebration where dancing and fireworks are in order, so drink up and be prepared to sing "yub nub" till dawn!

COCKTAIL DIFFICULTY: YOUNGLING
SERVES: 1
PREPARATION TIME: 5 MINUTES
GLASSWARE: COLLINS GLASS

3 ounces (90 milliliters)
smooth orange juice
1 ounce (30 milliliters)
triple sec
3 ounces (90 milliliters)
peach schnapps
ice cubes
Garnish: 1 wedge orange

/ In a cocktail shaker, combine the orange juice, triple sec, and peach schnapps in a Collins glass filled with ice cubes. Garnish with a small wedge of orange.

Wookiee & Cream Cocktail

The Wookiee & Cream Cocktail is the perfect dessert for any Star Wars super fan. With adorable Wookiee cookies hanging off the glass, guests will be roaring in excitement to get their paws on another!

COCKTAIL DIFFICULTY: JEDI MASTER
SERVES: 2
PREPARATION TIME: 3 HOURS
GLASSWARE: ROCKS GLASS

For the Rim
3 tablespoons chocolate sauce
3 tablespoons cookie crumbs from 1 Gingerbread Wookiee Cookie (recipe on page 86)

For the Cocktail
4 ounces (120 milliliters) white chocolate liqueur
4 ounces (120 milliliters) milk
2 ounces (60 milliliters) vanilla vodka
1 large scoop cookies and cream ice cream
Garnish: drizzle chocolate sauce and 1 Gingerbread Wookiee Cookie

/ For the rim, pour the chocolate sauce and cookie crumbs onto two separate shallow plates. Rim the martini glasses first in the chocolate sauce, then in the cookie crumbs (learn how to rim a glass on page 7).

/ For the cocktail, combine the white chocolate liqueur, milk, vanilla vodka, and a scoop of cookies and cream ice cream in a cocktail shaker, then shake until cool.

/ Drizzle chocolate sauce into the center of each martini glass. Pour the cocktail into the prepared glasses and garnish with a gingerbread Wookiee cookie.

Gingerbread Wookiee Cookies

SERVES: 20

3 cups (375 grams) plain flour

1 teaspoon baking soda

2 teaspoons cinnamon

1 teaspoon ginger

1 teaspoon salt

¾ cup (170 grams) butter, softened

¾ cup (150 grams) sugar

½ cup (165 grams) molasses

1 egg, lightly beaten

½ cup (90 grams) chocolate

¼ cup (45 grams) white chocolate chips

/ In a medium bowl, sift the flour and add in the baking soda, cinnamon, ginger, and salt. With an electric mixer, mix in the butter and sugar until the mix looks like bread crumbs.

/ Next, add in the molasses and egg and mix until well combined.

/ Tip the dough out, kneading briefly until smooth, then wrap in plastic wrap and leave to chill in the fridge for 15 minutes.

/ Preheat the oven to 350°F (180°C). Dust a smooth surface with flour and roll out a section of the dough to about ¼-inch thick. Use a gingerbread man cookie cutter or a knife to cut out your Wookiees.

/ Transfer to a baking tray and use a fork to imprint the "fur" into all of the cookie Wookiees.

/ Bake for 10 to 12 minutes or until lightly golden brown, then transfer to a wire rack to cool.

/ Once the cookies are cool, melt the chocolate, then transfer it into a piping bag and draw on a bandolier. Add white chocolate chips to the bandolier for a final flourish.

It's a Tasty Trap

Based on Admiral Ackbar's most famous Star Wars quote, this cocktail is the perfect drink to serve at your next Halloween party. Let it trick your guests with its vivid purple aesthetics; the last flavor people would expect is the strong citrus burst from the triple sec and orange concentrate.

COCKTAIL DIFFICULTY: JEDI KNIGHT
SERVES: 1
PREPARATION TIME: 5 MINUTES
GLASSWARE: MARTINI GLASS

1 ounce (30 milliliters) blue curaçao
1½ ounces (45 milliliters) triple sec
1 ounce (30 milliliters) cranberry juice
1 tablespoon orange concentrate
ice cubes
Garnish: 1 lemon wheel

/ In a cocktail shaker, combine the blue curaçao, triple sec, cranberry juice, and orange concentrate along with a handful of ice cubes. Shake until cool, then strain into a martini glass and garnish with a lemon wheel.

Mudhorn Mudslide

Jawas have always considered the Mudhorn's egg a delicious delicacy, which is definitely the case with this indulgent chocolate egg cocktail. Prepare to make the Mudhorn Mudslide your signature cocktail for any dinner party and, just like Baby Yoda, watch your guests levitate toward this chocolatey delight.

COCKTAIL DIFFICULTY: PADAWAN
SERVES: 1
PREPARATION TIME: 5 MINUTES
GLASSWARE: COUPE GLASS

1 ounce (30 milliliters) vodka

1 ounce (30 milliliters) coffee liqueur

1 ounce (30 milliliters) Irish cream

1½ ounces (45 milliliters) double cream

ice cubes

Garnish: chocolate shavings and 1 miniature chocolate egg

/ Combine the vodka, coffee liqueur, Irish cream, and double cream into a cocktail shaker with a handful of ice cubes and shake until cool.

/ Strain into a coupe glass and garnish with chocolate shavings and a miniature chocolate egg.

Mo-Greedo

Han Solo may have shot first, but in honor of Greedo, the ruthless bounty hunter, take a shot of this delicious green tea–infused mojito. Both refreshing and minty, to paraphrase Greedo himself, this is definitely a drink you will be looking forward to tasting for a long time.

COCKTAIL DIFFICULTY: PADAWAN
SERVES: 1
PREPARATION TIME: 5 MINUTES
GLASSWARE: COLLINS GLASS

½ cup (125 milliliters) green tea

2 tablespoons granulated sugar

several mint leaves

½ ounce (15 milliliters) fresh lime juice

½ lime, cut into wedges

ice cubes

1½ ounces (45 milliliters) light rum

Garnish: 1 lime slice and 1 mint sprig

/ Brew the green tea, then mix in the sugar and leave to cool.

/ In a Collins glass, muddle several mint leaves with the lime juice and lime wedges.

/ Next, fill the glass with ice cubes and add in the rum and cold green tea mix. Gently mix the drink with a bar spoon and garnish with a slice of lime and a mint sprig.

Sarlacc Surprise

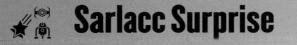

Straight from the Great Pit of Carkoon in the Dune Sea, this strong cocktail is a rumored favorite of Jabba the Hutt's. One of the stiffest drinks in the galaxy, with its strong combination of rye, absinthe, and bitters, this all-powerful cocktail should not be entered into lightly!

COCKTAIL DIFFICULTY: JEDI KNIGHT
SERVES: 1
PREPARATION TIME: 5 MINUTES
GLASSWARE: ROCKS GLASS

$\frac{1}{3}$ ounce (10 milliliters) absinthe

1 sugar cube

2$\frac{1}{3}$ ounces (70 milliliters) chilled water

3 dashes Peychaud's bitters

1 dash angostura bitters

$\frac{1}{3}$ ounce (20 milliliters) rye whiskey

$\frac{1}{3}$ ounce (20 milliliters) cognac

ice cube

Garnish: 1 lemon twist

/ Rinse a chilled rocks glass with absinthe and set aside.

/ In a mixing glass, muddle the sugar cube, water, and both bitters.

/ Add the rye and cognac, fill the mixing glass with ice, and stir until well-chilled. Strain into the prepared glass.

/ Twist the lemon peel over the drink's surface to extract the peel's oils, then garnish with the peel.

OUT-OF-THIS-WORLD COCKTAILS

The Outer Rim

The Outer Rim cocktail has all the beauty and wonder of the galaxy (and tastes out of this world, too)! Watch in astonishment as this drink changes color from blue to purple in front of your eyes while the edible glitter twinkles like the many stars scattered across space.

COCKTAIL DIFFICULTY: JEDI MASTER
SERVES: 1
PREPARATION TIME: 5 MINUTES
GLASSWARE: COUPE GLASS AND SHOT GLASS

salt, to rim glass
1¾ ounces (50 milliliters) tequila
⅞ ounce (25 milliliters) triple sec
2–3 tablespoons (10–15 drops) butterfly pea flower extract
pinch edible glitter
ice cubes
⅞ ounce (25 milliliters) fresh lemon juice

/ Rim a coupe glass with salt (learn how to rim a glass on page 7).

/ In a cocktail shaker, combine the tequila, triple sec, butterfly pea flower extract, and a pinch of edible glitter along with a handful of ice cubes.

/ Shake until cool, then strain into the rimmed coupe glass.

/ Next, squeeze the fresh lemon juice into a shot glass and, only when you want to show off the cocktail's color-changing properties, pour it in. (The butterfly pea flower extract works as a natural pH indicator and will react to the increase in acidity from the lemon juice by changing the color of the drink!)

The Naboo Taboo

As with Padmé and Anakin, we all know that when something is taboo, it becomes all the more tempting, so enhance your romantic fling with this gorgeous ombré cocktail.

COCKTAIL DIFFICULTY: JEDI KNIGHT
SERVES: 1
PREPARATION TIME: 5 MINUTES
GLASSWARE: HURRICANE GLASS

ice cubes
1½ ounces (45 milliliters) vodka
½ ounce (15 milliliters) peach schnapps
2 ounces (60 milliliters) smooth orange juice
2 ounces (60 milliliters) cranberry juice
Garnish: 1 lime wheel, 1 maraschino cherry, and pinch edible glitter

/ Fill a hurricane glass with ice cubes and gently layer in the vodka, peach schnapps, and orange and cranberry juices to achieve an orange-to-red ombré effect (see guidance on layering on page 7).

/ Top with a lime wheel, maraschino cherry, and a pinch of edible glitter to make this cocktail truly tempting.

Mos Espa Vesper

The Mos Espa Vesper is the best martini in the galaxy for sipping at a bar while watching all the shady characters coming and going. The sweetness from the vermouth perfectly offsets the slightly bitter notes of the dry gin, making this the smoothest cocktail in the Outer Rim!

COCKTAIL DIFFICULTY: PADAWAN
SERVES: 1
PREPARATION TIME: 5 MINUTES
GLASSWARE: MARTINI GLASS

2 ounces (60 milliliters) gin
¾ ounce (20 milliliters) vodka
½ ounce (15 milliliters) vermouth blanc
ice cubes
Garnish: 1 lemon twist

/ Combine the gin, vodka, and vermouth in a cocktail shaker along with a handful of ice cubes. Shake until cold and strain into a martini glass.

/ Twist a lemon peel over the drink's surface to extract the peel's oils, then garnish with the peel.

Tatooine Sunset

This intergalactic reboot of the classic Tequila Sunrise will have you longing to feel the sand beneath your toes on Skywalker's home planet. Add a miniature sparkler to really capture the magic of the twin golden sunset.

COCKTAIL DIFFICULTY: JEDI KNIGHT
SERVES: 1
PREPARATION TIME: 5 MINUTES
GLASSWARE: HURRICANE GLASS

2 teaspoons grenadine

1¾ ounces (50 milliliters) tequila

1 ounce (30 milliliters) triple sec

1 ounce (30 milliliters) fresh lemon juice

1 ounce (30 milliliters) fresh orange juice

ice cubes

Garnish: 1 orange wedge, 2 glacé cherries on a cocktail stick, and 1 miniature sparkler in a strawberry

/ Pour the grenadine into the base of a hurricane glass and set aside.

/ Combine the tequila, triple sec, and juices into a cocktail shaker with a handful of ice cubes. Shake vigorously until cool.

/ Add ice cubes into the hurricane glass, then carefully strain the cocktail, being careful not to disturb the grenadine layer.

/ Add more ice to fill the glass and garnish with an orange wedge and two glacé cherries on a cocktail stick. For the final flourish, secure a miniature sparkler in the strawberry and light before serving (see page 17 for safe use of sparklers). Remove and safely dispose of the spent sparkler before drinking!

Some Like It Hoth

This frozen delight captures the icy wonders of the planet Hoth perfectly. With a delicious blend of pineapple and coconut, this cocktail never fails to impress, so pour yourself a glass and keep toasty and warm (with or without the help of your own tauntaun!).

COCKTAIL DIFFICULTY: JEDI KNIGHT
SERVES: 1
PREPARATION TIME: 5 MINUTES
GLASSWARE: GOBLET GLASS

1 tablespoon maple or corn syrup, to rim glass

desiccated coconut, to rim glass

crushed ice

2 ounces (60 milliliters) pineapple juice

1 ounce (30 milliliters) blue curaçao

1 ounce (30 milliliters) vodka

1 ounce (30 milliliters) cream of coconut

/ Rim a goblet glass with maple or corn syrup and desiccated coconut (learn how to rim a glass on page 7).

/ In a blender, combine crushed ice with the pineapple juice, blue curaçao, vodka, and cream of coconut. Blend the mixture until smooth and serve in your prepared glass.

The Dagobah's Grasshopper

Don't let the vivid green color of this cocktail unnerve you; hidden beneath the swamp of mint leaves is a delicious mint candy flavor. The perfect drink to continue your training in mastering mixology while connecting to the deeper cosmic Force of the universe.

COCKTAIL DIFFICULTY: PADAWAN
SERVES: 1
PREPARATION TIME: 5 MINUTES
GLASSWARE: MARTINI GLASS

¾ ounce (23.5 milliliters)
  Crème de Cacao
¾ ounce (23.5 milliliters)
  Crème de Menthe
¾ ounce (23.5 milliliters)
  single cream
ice cubes
Garnish: 1 mint leaf

/ Combine the Crème de Cacao, Crème de Menthe, and single cream into a cocktail shaker with a handful of ice cubes. Shake until cool.

/ Strain the cocktail into a martini glass and garnish with a mint leaf.

Coruscant Cosmopolitan

The Coruscant Cosmopolitan is the quintessential cocktail for any big night out. Full of excitement from popping candy and flying saucers, this sweet treat is the perfect cocktail to set off a memorable night on the town!

COCKTAIL DIFFICULTY: PADAWAN
SERVES: 1
PREPARATION TIME: 5 MINUTES
GLASSWARE: MARTINI GLASS

popping candy, to rim glass
1½ ounces (45 milliliters) lemon vodka
½ ounce (15 milliliters) triple sec
½ ounce (15 milliliters) fresh lime juice
1 ounce (30 milliliters) cranberry juice
ice cubes
Garnish: flying saucers candy on a cocktail stick

/ Rim a martini glass with popping candy (learn how to rim a glass on page 7).

/ Combine the vodka, triple sec, and juices into a cocktail shaker along with a handful of ice cubes. Shake until cold and strain into the martini glass.

/ Garnish with a few flying saucers candy on a cocktail stick. The candy will dissolve into the cocktail when stirred.

Bespin Breeze

Let all your problems float away after a few sips of this cloud city—inspired cocktail. This rose-infused cocktail is light and breezy with its perfect foam and cotton candy garnish.

COCKTAIL DIFFICULTY: JEDI MASTER
SERVES: 1
PREPARATION TIME: 5 MINUTES
GLASSWARE: COUPE GLASS

1 ounce (30 milliliters)
   rose-infused gin
½ ounce (15 milliliters)
   Crème de Cacao
⅓ ounce (10 milliliters)
   fresh lemon juice
⅓ ounce (10 milliliters)
   rose water
1 egg white
ice cubes
Garnish: 1 cotton candy cloud

/ Combine all ingredients in a cocktail shaker and shake until cool.

/ Strain the cocktail into a coupe glass and garnish with a cotton candy cloud.

STAR WARS DRINKING GAME

This Star Wars-fueled drinking game is based on one of the galaxy's best, Ring of Fire. You will need a tall glass, a deck of cards, and copious cocktails to play!

How to Play

Place a tall glass in the middle of a table. Surround the glass with a circle of cards facing down. All players must be divided into two teams: the light side and the dark side. Take it in turn to draw a card from the deck, with each card having a specific task assigned to it:

Ace: Pod race
Race to finish downing your drink, waterfall style. You can't stop drinking until the person next to you decides to stop.

2: Perform a Jedi mind trick!
Choose someone to take a drink.

3. Talk like Yoda, you must!
Talk like Yoda and invert every sentence until the next person picks up a two. Failure to do so results in having to finish your drinks. As the Master once said, "do or do not, there is no try!"

4. Light side
All those on the light side must take a drink.

5. Dark side
All those on the dark side must take a drink.

6. It's a trap!
Everyone takes a drink!

7. Young Padawan
Pick someone to be your padawan and teach them the Jedi way of drinking. They drink every time you do.

8. Jar Jar Blinks
Challenge someone to a staring contest. Whoever blinks first must drink!

9. Get Sith-faced
Anyone wearing black or red must take a drink.

10. Resist the dark side!
This card triggers a "never have I ever" confession from the person who picked the card. All those who have done the action in question must drink.

Jack: Jedi council
As a member of the Jedi council, you must make a rule. Anyone who disobeys must be punished severely . . . by taking a drink!

Queen: The Emperor
Until the next Queen is picked up, you are the Emperor, and anyone who does not refer to you as such must take a drink.

King: The sauce is strong with you . . .
Contribute a third of your drink to the central glass. Whoever picks up the fourth and final King must succumb to the dark side and down the contents of that glass.

CONVERSION CHART

Term	Measurement (Imperial)	Measurement (Metric)
1 part	Any equal part	Any equal part
1 dash	$^1/_{32}$ ounce	1 milliliter
1 teaspoon	$^1/_5$ ounce	6 milliliters
1 tablespoon	$^1/_6$ ounce	5 milliliters
1 pony	½ ounce	15 milliliters
1 jigger/shot	1 ounce	30 milliliters
1 snit	3 ounces	90 milliliters
1 wine glass	4 ounces	120 milliliters
1 split	6 ounces	180 milliliters
1 cup	8 ounces	240 milliliters
1 pint	16 ounces	475 milliliters

INDEX

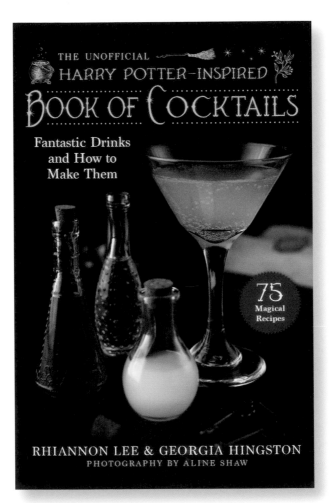